AF454339

Songs

Of the

Soul

By

Edward Lee McDaniel

Contents

Introduction

Welcome to Edward's World!

A place of my thoughts and sentiments are put into words.

A place where I speak for the unsung voices and the unheard.

Keep your head up.

Keep hopes alive.

Don't lose faith and don't lose control.

Welcome to the Songs Of My Soul

My Daddy's Shoes

I've been living my life,

Paying my dues,

The ancestors stand with me.

My feet may never fill my daddy's shoes,

I find myself coasting through the ups and downs of reality,

I know part of his legacy lives on in me,

I could never be the man he was.

He instilled many of his values within me,

Sometimes I wonder did the apple fall far from the tree;

He was a man of great knowledge,

He made sure he provided for mom and me,

Even if it meant he had taken less.

No matter how bad things got,

He never gave up his faith in the Lord,

It's not easy living in this world,

There is always someone trying to catch you off guard.

I just want to be a better man.

I ask God to protect me and help me through the things I don't

understand,

I know he has a plan,

I find myself letting my imagination run away with me,

Writing these musings in my diary,

I can only hold myself accountable for my own actions,

Other people's actions are out of my control.

Daddy would polish up those Stacy Adams shoes,

Hold his head up high walk tall and proud;

His voice was loud,

He could attract a crowd,

He could wear a casual suit and sneakers,

He looked like a million dollars when he rocked his executive suit and

boots.

He never forgot his roots many times I get overwhelmed,

It's people out here that don't care what they say or do,

Them be the main ones watching you,

How would you feel about every choice I make?

Certain mess you would not take.

You didn't mind helping others,

If it would make a difference, you would give the shirt off of your back.

I remember daddy prayed for me to have the gift of speech,

Next thing you know I'm writing poems and raps,

I could never fill my daddy's shoes.

He loved Doo Wops and classic rhythm and blues,

I still listen to many of the classics he introduced me to,

Every time I play that music, I think of you.

So many people get caught up in the mess and miss the message,

So busy pointing fingers at each other that you miss out on your

blessings.

Daddy was aware of the strikes against him because of the color of his

skin,

He pushed himself to the absolute maximum,

He was a great man who always aspired to be greater;

He was a math whiz he didn't need a calculator,

He had a special intuition to feel when something was not right.

Even though there was a lot of darkness in the world he was a light,

I know God, him, and mom are watching over me from heaven,

Cheering me on through the good,

Protecting and shielding me from the bad,

I was truly blessed to have such a wonderful mom and dad,

He lived his life well and paid his dues,

I'm yet to meet a man who can fill my daddy's shoes.

I Really Miss My Momma

Mother's Day is not the same without you;

You always knew what to say and do.

My mom was very special,

She knew how to make everything alright.

I remember when I was a little boy,

She would tuck me in at night,

She would pray with me so I wouldn't be restless she read me Psalms 23,

After that I would calm down, turn off the lights and go to sleep.

In the morning, she would cook breakfast sausage, eggs, toast, and

cheese served with orange juice or hot sweet tea;

I would go outside to play after I would eat,

I loved my momma she would tell me to stay out of trouble and I would

obey.

She would look out the window when I was outside to make sure I was

okay,

I loved playing in the water as a kid I once had a plastic pool.

Time rolled on and it was time for me to go to school,

Head start was nice, and kindergarten was cool,

I remember we had mats and would take naps in school.

Me and mother and father lived comfortably we were not rich,

We moved from number 4 to number 7,

She warned me to stay out of the ditch.

I had a hard head and went in the ditch anyway until one day when I

saw a giant black snake,

I ran in the house so fast that day you would have thought,

I was an Olympic runner;

The snakes must have liked the water in the ditch and the shade when it

was hot in the summer,

Looking back at that day, I must have been out my mind,

That was the end of my playing in the ditch time.

I learned my lesson that day,

Always listen to what momma and daddy say,

If you disobey you better be ready to face the consequences that come

your way.

My momma was a phenomenal woman like Michelle Obama,

She was a nice lady that did not like drama,

She loved the Lord and going to church on Sunday.

This poem is dedicated to my momma,

Rest in Love, Happy Mother's Day.

Don't Give Up

Trials and tribulations are going to happen,

Don't give up! Don't Give Up!

Friends are going to turn to foes,

Don't Give Up! Don't Give Up!

Doors will open and doors will close,

Don't Give Up! Don't Give Up!

No matter what they do to you or what they say,

Don't give up, you are going to make it anyway.

Friends long gone, family is too,

Don't Give Up! Don't Give Up!

Sitting at home all alone, the four walls and you,

Don't Give Up! Don't Give Up!

Times are hard and it's hard to cope,

Don't Give Up! Don't Give Up!

God is sending you signs to give you hope;

I refuse to lose; I refuse to just stand down,

I refuse to be a hopeless victim,

Wallowing in my misery and self-pity,

Hope is not lost; God is my hope.

I refuse to listen to those negative voices in my head,

Negative voices telling me I will not achieve,

I will achieve, I shall achieve because I believe.

I have the ability to turn my dreams into reality,

This is my hope from me to you; this is my testimony;

Storms and struggles going to come,

Storms and struggles going to go,

You see, storms and struggles are the building blocks

of life that enable us to grow.

If we believe, we can achieve we speak good things into existence in our

lives.

Sometimes we have to turn a bad song into a good song;

Make what's wrong right.

You see it starts within us we must search our own hearts.

It takes persistence and willpower to be able to finish what you start;

People laugh at you and talk crazy,

Don't Give Up! Don't Give Up!

Plotting and scheming but it just doesn't faze me,

Don't Give Up! Don't Give Up!

You see the hope is inside us,

Like the rose that grew from the concrete.

Through God and our knowledge of self,

We are able to safely swim those waters that are cold and deep,

We can climb those mountains, no matter how high;

I believe in God, I believe in me,

The devil is a lie,

Don't Give Up! Don't Give Up!

I see my future and it's looking really bright,

I'm prepared to past this test and survive this long dark night,

Don't Give Up! Don't Give Up!

I've never been a quitter,

So why on Earth would I choose to quit now?

I have faith, strong self-esteem, and knowledge of self, that's how.

The negativity and negative voices only push me closer to my

constellation,

I turn all that hating into my motivation,

You see, I love it when you lie looking me dead in the eyes,

I don't give up, I haven't failed yet that's the reason why.

My spirit is too strong and so is my willpower,

My strong mentality is on a whole other level,

I won't give up so you can put that in your pipe and smoke it devil,

Don't Give Up!

Time Is Ticking Away

When I wake up in the morning,

I'm grateful to see another day.

Life is precious time is ticking away,

You never know when the sand in your hourglass

Is going to run dry,

When I think about my loved ones

I've lost it makes me cry.

I have no time to waste,

I'm living my best life every moment,

Everything that I'm proud of, I own it.

Another day is an opportunity to get it right,

Soaring to new heights,

I don't want to be good,

I want to be great.

I pour my heart and soul into everything I create;

Possibilities are endless as long as I put my best foot forward and try.

I'm not going to let other people's words determine how I am defined;

I'm going to let my gift make a way for me.

Let my light shine;

I will continue to give every effort my best,

No half stepping is allowed,

I'm going to make my parents proud.

It was my dream to be a writer

Since I was a child;

I will continue to push my pen,

Raising my profile,

I'm going to bring heat I will not bring slaw.

If I can do this, anyone can.

It all began in Helena, Arkansas;

God willing bigger and better things will come my way,

Time is not standing still,

Time is ticking away.

If I Was A Storm Chaser

Imagine if I was a storm chaser,

I'm a writer I give ideas with my pen,

I get rid of what I don't like with my eraser,

What if I chased wall clouds and funnel clouds like Tim Reed.

Imagine me driving up and down the interstates with speed,

My adrenaline pumping feeling appreciated because my services are

needed,

It takes a lot to be taken seriously.

I want to see and do more, so I explore,

That's my curiosity.

I could have been a basketball player,

I could have been a football player,

I could have been a bull rider,

I decided to be a creative writer.

Real life events get me inspired,

I'll write poetry until the day I ride off into the sunset and lay my pen

down forever.

When I was young, I wanted to show you the radar and give you the

weather forecast.

I used to have a barometer, humidity meter, and a rain gauge,

Studying the weather was once my dream.

I have a huge appreciation for storm chasers maybe one day I can ride

along on a storm chase with Tim Reed,

I could be on TV,

We could talk about weather storm chasing and poetry.

Easter

Easter is the time of year when we celebrate the resurrection of Christ,

He gave his life for our sins, he paid the ultimate price.

A time of joy, happiness, worship, and peace.

We celebrate with bright colored suits, prayer, praise, worship, and feast,

We honor the Lord with worship songs we sing.

Remembering when those poor mere mortals sacrificed their king.

Years later, we are still singing and dancing in the rain,

He is still the king of all kings, he still reigns,

He is the Most High.

When I think of that day it makes me cry,

Everyone wearing their Sunday bests,

Thank you, God, for bringing me through life's storms and tests,

I'm still a work in progress I must confess;

Thank you for all you have done for me you are the best.

He knows our heart and our intentions,

Don't be weary, worry, or stress,

He always works things out for the best.

What a wonderful day we woke up in the land of the living,

We are blessed and highly favored for real,

Such an awesome God we serve, he gives us our hearts desires as long as

it is in his will.

He gives us abundance so much more than we deserve,

My faith in Christ is worth more than silver and gold.

He's the only one who can give me eternal life and save my soul.

My Sweet Gem

I was a lost teddy bear,

My sweet gem found me.

She brought me up after everyone else,

Had brought me down,

She helped me see my potential.

She motivates me helping me build up my confidence,

To do things I never thought I could do,

My sweet gem, I'm so in love with you.

If I had never met you, I would still be lost in this world,

She was sent by an angel,

She changed my life, I'm so lucky to have her as my girl.

I thank God for her, the true love of my life,

She's my better half, my lucky charm.

We are together forever, arm in arm,

She has my back through the life's storms,

She is no fly by night, she is by my side to stay.

I'm so glad she is here to chase the clouds away,

She never gives up on me,

She's my lover and my best friend.

As long as I have my sweet gem,

I'm overjoyed with laughter over and over again.

My Sweet Love

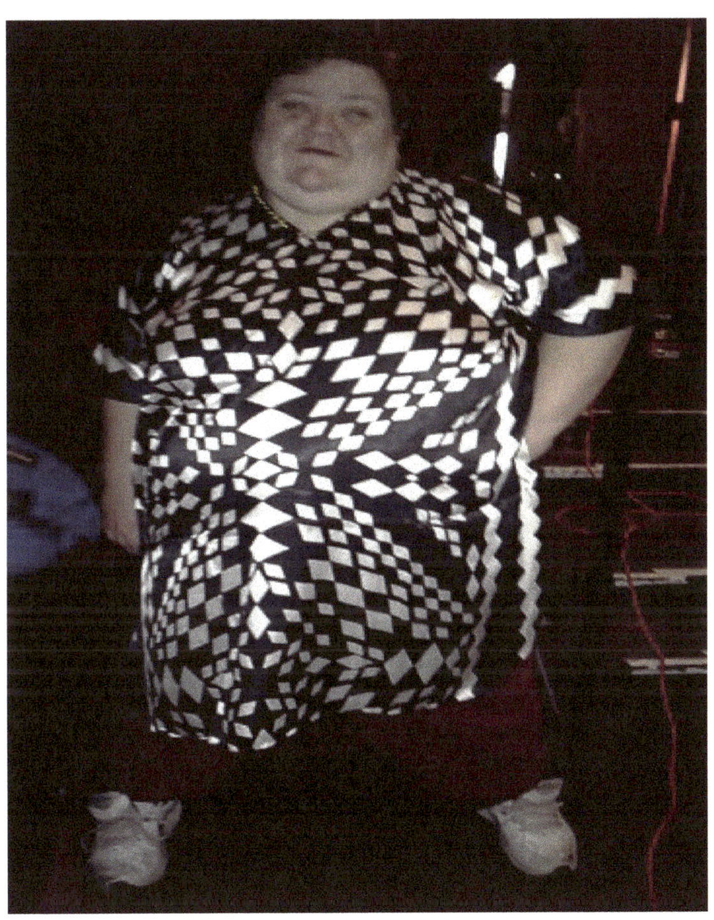

My sweet love has been by my side,

Through the highs and the lows.

The cup of our love like the river still flows,

After many tests of time, we are still together.

Having you in my life forever,

Our soul tie is too strong to ever be severed.

Every moment with you, I cherish and savor,

You keep my life from tasting bland, you give it flavor.

I have the world in the palm of my hands as long as I have you,

Even on cloudy days you turn my grey skies blue.

Together we make the best of every situation,

When I'm feeling down you encourage me with motivation.

I know God sent you in my life from up above,

Until the end of time, I'm going to stand by my sweet love.

Having you by my side, I can't go wrong,

If I could sing a tune, I would write you a love song.

I cherish every measure of our life,

Together, we enjoy the bitter and sweet cup.

Through the good times and when times get rough,

We have a bond that will never be broken.

Through life, we are smooth sailing,

Like a ship in the ocean,

Going through the motions.

I love her from the bottom of my heart,

I knew she was the one for me from the very start,

We are together forever, our love shall never part.

Guardian Angels

This is dedicated to all of the people,

I've lost over the years.

I've shed so many tears,

I lived through some of my biggest fears coming true.

Things have not been the same since my pops been gone,

I miss him giving me advice and encouragement.

I remember when he would give me situation's report on the phone,

People showed me how they really felt about me.

True colors were shown,

I had to open my eyes to see the bigger picture,

Now I'm looking at life from a different angle.

The people who I lost are now my guardian angels,

Watching over me with the Lord,

Sending me warning signs when I'm in danger.

We have to be careful who we allow in our space,

Sometimes the ones we think we know can be more dangerous

to us than dealing with a complete stranger,

That is why we are told to walk in faith and not in sight.

After losing mom and dad I learned to cherish and appreciate life,

I change the things I can and accept the things I cannot change.

I've outgrown a lot of people I was once close to.

When my mom went home to the Lord,

I found out who my friends really were.

From the people didn't care if I sink or swim,

I felt numb things looked grim.

I didn't even have time to grieve and heal properly,

My apartment manager switched up on me.

I was evicted out of my apartment,

For six months I lived in my car,

Homeless on the streets,

Thank God for soup kitchens and good friends I never went a day

without eating.

Through it all I learned a valuable lesson,

It was time for relocation.

There was a dark cloud hanging over me blocking my blessings,

I left Memphis I really didn't have a plan.

I stepped out on faith,

I was not going to wait,

I refused to surrender to depression,

Things turned around in the blink of an eye,

God Is always able, the devil Is a lie.

I know my guardian angels are smiling,

Celebrating my blessings up above,

It's been a long and winding road.

I couldn't have survived without God's mercy, protection, and favor,

I couldn't have survived without love.

Red Cardinal

When I see a red cardinal outside of my window, I know my loved one is

nearby,

I know you are looking out for me,

I often think about you as I watch different cloud formations in the sky.

You are so beautiful made from love,

You are a sign of hope from heaven above,

You wish me much success, joy, and happiness,

You love me at my worst and at my best.

I'm going to get a bird feeder so when you stop by again you can have a

bite to eat.

When a red cardinal stops by my window,

It makes my day complete.

I feel your positive energy,

You are always full of cheer,

You come and visit all through the year.

Such a lovely bird of fire symbolizing growth and change,

Everything is happening as it should, it's all in the game.

I know God is with me when I see a red cardinal outside of my window,

I look forward to what lies ahead I'm watching and waiting.

All things happen in due time I must stay calm and exercise patience.

Oh, beautiful red cardinal bird of fire bird of light,

I received such a sweet messenger from heaven I must be doing

something right.

The Mischievous Raccoon

Once there was a raccoon that was always getting into trouble,

He would always find a way to pop your bubble.

He never would leave well enough alone,

He kept pressing his luck until something went wrong.

This mischievous raccoon was young and restless always into something,

He had a hard head he was a know it all, you could not tell him nothing.

I would go the opposite way when I see him coming,

Anything that could go wrong would go wrong around him.

He was destructive anything he touched would break,

If you let him borrow your stuff that would be your biggest mistake.

I remember once he stuck a pencil in a light bulb socket,

It lit up like the 4th of July, I thought it was a rocket.

That raccoon would not stop it,

He would go in people's garbage and make a mess.

I always wondered why he had to be such a pain in the behind and a pest.

That little mischievous raccoon was such a clown,

If he doesn't learn to behave himself, they are going to run him out of town.

Trouble is always around the corner when that raccoon comes around,

You do too much, I can't keep being your friend I'm going to have to put you down.

When A Child Is Born

Children are born innocent,

When they come into the world,

Their mind is a clean slate.

It's very important we teach them to love and not hate.

If we want them to grow into responsible adults,

We have to make sure we train them the right way.

Remember, they pick up every word the people around them say,

Watch what you and others do around them; what they see you do they

will emulate.

You have to set ground rules for them to obey,

Let them know what's acceptable and what's not ok.

Show them love and listen to what they have to say,

Let them be innocent with their toys and play,

Let children stay in a children's place.

Don't let them grow up too fast,

Keep them around other children and out of grown folk's face

We have to hold ourselves to a higher standard if we want our children

to have great integrity and character.

The way we raise our children will determine the future of America.

Teach them to use their head and not do everything they see,

If I had children, I would want my children to be better than me.

Painting Words on a Blank Canvas

We use our words like a paintbrush,

Awakening the masses from their deep sleep.

Words of encouragement,

We search for the silver lining,

We chase the darkness away the sun is shining.

The ancestors stand with us,

Through our words, we give them justice due,

My words resonate with you,

Maybe you've been through similar situations too.

I can remember times when it felt like

My world was coming to an end,

When I didn't have no one to talk to but God,

Long gone were my family and friends,

I found writing as a release,

I put my words on a page,

One day, I was handed a flyer inviting me to

Mot & Ed's Open Mic Night, it was like cool a place,

I can say my poetry on stage.

I kept my pen sharp and got better with my writing,

I would step on stage and shut it down like Tennessee Titan.

Life was handing me lemons,

I was furious,

Finally, I found a platform,

Where people took me seriously.

I knew I had to take my writing career further,

Miss Edna made the very best stuffed turkey burgers.

I met many great artists in the local talent scene, many connections were

made;

Expressing myself was food to my soul,

Sugar to my Kool-Aid,

The pen is my brush.

I let my soul speak.

People don't always have time to talk,

I'm like alright then,

I grab my notebook and speak through my pen,

My safe space where I can say what I need to say,

I write my troubles away,

It helps me find beauty and run off the beast,

Painting words on a blank canvas is how I find peace.

Summertime

Summer is my favorite time of the year,

Honeysuckles smell so sweet,

Wasp and bees buzzing around.

I'm sipping on lemonade in the shade,

Trying to beat the heat

It's a beautiful day to take a ride downtown,

Look at the sites and listen to the systems pound,

We can hang out at the park and chill out in the parking spot,

Take a walk under the tree and sit on the bench.

I have soda pops and water to keep our thirst quenched,

The park is crowded people are walking their dogs,

Barbecuing on the grill,

I'm seeing people I haven't seen in years,

I just came here to chill.

Clear blue skies not a drop of rain in sight,

It's summertime in the city and I'm feeling alright.

Everyone is dressed comfortably the park looks like a car exhibit,

People take pride in their rides you can look but you better not hit it.

We are having a party, I hope the police don't shut us down,

This is how we do it in Helena town.

I'm chilling in my Chevy over the levee,

That's where I will be.

Everybody trying to get my attention by blowing their horns even

walking in front of my car to speak,

What's up MC. Lee?

Everything is good what has been up.

Pouring my cranberry juice into my Styrofoam cup,

This is something you would expect to see on TV.

A big crowd of people gathered as far as the eyes can see,

It looks like a big family reunion.

I hope nobody doesn't start shooting,

Chilling down in the delta the home of the blues.

Where our great ancestors worked the land and paid their dues,

A beautiful summer day to get out and about,

It's summertime in the delta in the deep south.

Ghetto Queen

She is a beautiful flower,

Born and raised in the ghetto,

No one knows the trouble,

Her eyes have seen,

She's too strong to be held down,

She is a ghetto queen.

She knows the streets,

Her game is tight,

She's smoking on Mary Jane, feeling alright.

She's very active in the community,

She's very talented; she can sing like a bird.

If you are a square, she will kick you to the curb,

She is about her hustle to her money talks,

Bull must take a walk.

If you waste her time, she will tell you to get lost,

She is her own boss,

She is ghetto fabulous in her clothes,

She can take care of herself any way the wind blows.

Her feet pound the pavement,

She kicks up dirt,

She is a pit bull in a skirt.

If you waste her time and play with her money.,

You will get your feelings hurt.

She is as sweet as a kitten,

She has a heart of gold,

She has rhythm and a lot of soul,

She takes a little and makes it go a long way,

She cherishes each day, she loves the Lord, and she prays every day.

Each day she works her magic,

When she comes on the scene,

You will put some respect on her name,

She is a proud ghetto queen.

Give People Their Flowers While They Are Here

We have to start showing appreciation to our loved ones while they are

living

Every day we wake up,

We should act like it's Thanksgiving,

Remind people how special they are to you.

All of our time is borrowed,

Tell them today no one is guaranteed a tomorrow,

Tomorrow could be too late,

Let them know today don't wait.

We must learn to swallow our foolish pride,

Make our feelings known, not hold them inside.

Through the years, so many people,

Have went home,

It don't cost nothing to check on your people give them a call, pick up

the phone.

Doesn't anyone do simple wellness checks anymore?

Or do they only get in contact when they need something or when

something is wrong?

Don't wait until it's too late when they are gone they are gone,

Give people their flowers while they are here,

Keep in touch with your loved ones far and near,

You never know when it's going to be the last time.

So, make sure you show appreciation and love to your loved ones,

Make sure they are OK and feeling fine,

Blood is thicker than water, a simple encouraging word will do,

Remind them they are a part of you.

When it comes to foolishness,

We do the most,

Let's take some of that time and energy to celebrate the ones we hold

close to our heart,

When it comes to family we should have unconditional love.

Life continues on living, sometimes things get rough,

It gets so tough it will make you feel like

Your very best is not good enough.

You can talk to me anytime you are feeling stressed or depressed,

I will do my best to cheer you up,

This is life we have to sip every measure of its bitter and sweet cup,

We have to find a reason to smile even when things are messed up.

I want to give my loved ones their flowers while they are here,

I want them to know to my heart they are dear,

I wish them all the best life has to offer,

May all of their dreams and ambitions come true.

Dear family friends and loved ones,

I want you to know Edward loves you.

I've Got to Have You

Oh, what I wouldn't do to kiss your lips,

Rub through your thighs and caress your hips,

Yes, I would do just about anything in the world,

Just to have a fine beautiful girl.

I've climbed the highest mountain,

Swimmer the deepest sea,

Still, I cannot find the one that's for me.

I need a friend first, we must have something in common,

We must be compatible I don't need no drama,

I need someone I can grow older with,

Live life to the fullest together.

We can make it through tough times and rough weather,

When it's storming outside, we have peace where it matters the most.

I need your sweetness in my life like I love,

Cinnamon on my French Toast,

You ask me am I ready for love,

I'd say yes, I need someone that brings out my best.

My past conquests must have been touched in the head,

It's more to a relationship than laying in the bed.

You have to captivate each other's mind,

Do activities together keep it exciting?

Otherwise, there will be disturbances thunder and lightning.

I want us to go places together taking vacations,

I want us to lift up each other,

Not tearing each other down.

I'm talking about elevation,

We can listen to the radio,

We can watch TV,

It's all good as long as you are here with me.

Let's enjoy ourselves go out to a restaurant to eat,

Or we can go to the movies or watch a concert and listen to the vocal and

the beat,

As long as you are with me, my missing link is complete.

I will make sure I treat you right,

All the other girls will have to take a seat.

You satisfy my sweet tooth like a Laffy taffy,

As long as I have you, I am happy.

You are the spice of my life,

The sun in my sky,

I knew I had to have you the day you walked by.

She's A Good Girl

She's a good girl,

She is not a faker,

As real as it gets as lovely as Dorothy Dandridge,

As sexy as Josephine Baker.

She is a welcomed site for sore eyes to see,

What must I do to get this beautiful damsel to come

home with me.

I can be your moon and stars,

Let me light up your world.

She has grace and style,

She drives men wild,

Like Marilyn Monroe,

She has a million-dollar smile,

A Beyonce and a Barbara Streisand of her time,

She is in her prime.

Her radiant light shines,

She is a trendsetter blowing minds,

Sensitive about her stuff like Erykah Badu,

I just want to put this teddy bear passion on you.

I'll have you hooked, your exhaust will be steaming,

You will have to pinch yourself to make sure,

You are not dreaming.

I aim to please, satisfaction is guaranteed,

I'm doing my best to make you see what is meant to be,

We should be a reality not a make believe,

I long for your sweet nectar like a bumblebee.

You are my Miley Cyrus,

You are my sunshine,

When I think of you, I hear ocean waves crashing.

My Madonna, my Janet Jackson,

Your strong presence is a gift,

My Selena Gomez, my Taylor Swift.

You are not a fly by night,

You are here to stay,

She is on her champagne tip like Janelle Monae,

Like a child on a playground I just want to go play.

You give me a spiritual awakening like Writeous Soul,

She has that natural beauty like Poetic Flo,

A plus size queen like Lizzo and Dassia Rose,

She makes the best stuffed turkey burgers like Miss Edna.

She's a go getter,

She is on her Nicki Minaj and on her Cardi B,

She is my missing link,

She is very pretty in pink.

She knows how to change my oil and make my battleship sink,

Come and walk the red carpet with me,

Help me conquer all of my fears,

My Vivica A. Fox, my Foxy Brown, my Jennifer Lopez, my Britney Spears.

My heart goes on for you my Celine Dion,

My word is bond,

You launch my rocket into outer space,

I can't wait for you to feel my bass.

When we come together it's lights, camera, action,

We are poetry in motion we are never lacking,

Such a beautiful rose with a nice thorn,

My Nina Simone, my Lena Horn.

She's my Southern Belle and my Northern Lights,

She came into my life to love me right,

My Tonya Dyson, my Natalie Cole, my Jordan Sparks.

We love to kick it after dark,

My news reporter my Norah O Connell, my Jerika Duncan,

My sweet little munchkin with the junk in the trunk.

When we met it was an instant attraction,

She unbreaks my heart like Toni Braxton,

I proceed in her direction with ease,

I keep on falling in love with her like Alicia Keys.

She soothes my soul leaving me fulfilled,

I feel good all over like Stephanie Mills,

I'm her man I bring home the bacon,

She is a sexy red girl like Sanaa Lathan.

She's my friend until the end,

She's living proof a broken heart can mend.

Underneath This Poet's Sky

A plethora of thoughts running through my mind,

Through the break in the clouds comes the sunshine,

I wonder what mystery awaits me outside of these gates.

I'm living inside of a dream,

I take it day by day I must trust the process.

Embracing my journey and any inconveniences,

I may face a temporary setback,

I will not allow that to cause me to take a whole step back,

I must keep my eyes on the road.

Using my peripheral vision,

I take nothing for granted each day,

I'm very thankful to still be in the land of the living.

Everyone is fighting their own battles,

Everything is not about you,

Don't take everything so personal.

The skyline is vast,

I'm vibrating on a higher frequency,

I'm not giving into negativity.

When trouble comes my way, I walk away and laugh,

I'm staying in my own lane maintaining self-control over my own vehicle,

I don't want to crash.

Life happens really fast in the blink of an eye,

The game changes.

People you grew up with and knew for years start acting like complete strangers,

People who used to be your friends start acting like your foes,

You just have to be prepared for whichever way the wind blows.

I'm trying to reach elevation, I rock steadily.

The sun shines and the stars in the cosmos sing in harmony,

I join in with my keyboard and play a beautiful bass line rhythm track and melody.

I'm not going to let these trials and tribulations get the best of me,

I've found some pills to be hard to swallow,

I'm not going to let nothing get the best of me,

I refuse to drown in a sea of misery and wallow,

I'm living me best life today,

Just in case there is no tomorrow.

I'm through wasting time,

I have no more time to procrastinate,

You want to see my passion for poetry, give me an opportunity to demonstrate,

My words will hit you so hard,

You have to fall back and let it marinate.

I don't gargle my words I fully enunciate,

I should have been a teacher minds, I stimulate,

Through poetry I educate.

When I signed up for this, I stepped out the boat and took a leap of

faith,

God doesn't make no mistakes,

Whatever the future holds for me I'm so anxious,

Too see my dreams come to fruition,

I know I must be patient but I can't wait.

Like Caged Bird

I know what it feels like to be trapped,

Like a bird in a cage,

Wishing to be free someday to fly away,

Confined to a small space where right now,

My only escape is to use my imagination.

These four walls are full of isolation,

I'm still held responsible for the contents,

Inside my station when these steel doors finally open up,

I'll be free as a bird walking out of here a new man after graduation.

You don't have to be incarcerated to be locked up. you can be restricted

in free society,

You can be a prisoner of depression and anxiety.

Your wings could have been clipped by someone or something.

Have you ever wondered what makes a caged bird sing?

Imagine a person that's been oppressed their whole life finally

experiencing what having freedom can bring.

When the cage opens fly little birdie you will be free to fly,

You were born a warrior real G's don't die.

They can take away your money, they can take away your most prized

possessions

But don't you ever let them take away your dignity and your pride.

You are like the ugly duckling, the underdog, the one least likely to succeed,

You hold the key to your own destiny,

I'm no longer trapped inside this cage in my mind,

I am free.

BBQ Chicken Wings

Last night I had some of the best BBQ Chicken Wings,

They were dripping with sauce,

They were so good I was online and had to get off.

I was happy eating those chicken wings like a kid in a candy store,

When I got done I wanted some more.

It took my mind off of all the foolishness and drama,

It took me back to the times when I would have dinner with my mama.

Those wings were fit for a king or president,

I'm talking Bill Clinton, George Bush, Barack Obama,

So good they could get a praise dance out your grandmama.

If you want to make up with your significant other make sure you serve them some chicken wings

Smothered in sauce like the ones I had last night,

Those wings will make you forget about whatever made you argue or fight.

They will taste those juicy BBQ Chicken Wings make peace and love you right.

I believe those BBQ Chicken Wings could squash all beef and bring about world peace.

I felt on top of the world like I was a boss, I was on cloud nine eating those BBQ chicken wings dripping in sauce.

How Long

How long are we going to continue to make the same mistakes over and
over again,
People out here sewing dragon seeds and not expecting to reap the
world's wind,
You reap exactly what you sew.
We are all adults we should know better how long are we going to
pretend like we don't know which way to go,
I call out ignorance and disrespect.
I come in peace; I don't care for confrontation,
But if you cross the line I will put you in check.
When you don't speak up people think you are giving them a pass and
saying it's ok,
You will give me respect and when you address me you will watch what
you say.
How long will we remain in denial when will we accept the truth and see
what's right in front of our face?
How long will I be made to feel out of place?
Seems like forever that I've been running around in this rat race,
Some people change some people stay the same.
You ask the average person they'll tell you it's all in the game,
How low will you stoop for clout or fame?
What an embarrassment you are to our kind,

You had an opportunity to make us proud, instead you put us to shame.

How long will we repeat this vicious cycle is it a generational curse?

You can straighten up and fly right or end up in a hearse,

How long are we going to keep each other down and talk behind one

another's backs?

We used to be friends remember back in the days when my parents took

us to McDonald's, bought us a large soda large fries and a Big Mac,

Now we behave like we don't know how to act.

You used to be so intelligent; what the hell happened did you start

smoking crack?

What kind of a friend would laugh about another friend getting jacked?

Them are not your friends them people are wack.

How long must this go on?

How can we be strong if we continue to do each other wrong?

We ought to be tired of singing the same song but we continue to allow

this mess to go on.

A Hood News Reporter

I'm a poet like a hood news reporter,

Telling you about things I've been through experienced and seen,

I wish reality could be different.

Through the years it's like we've been singing the same songs people still

doing the same things,

I feel like a broken record,

Saying the same things over and over again.

Sometimes I don't know where to begin,

When will these injustices end?

When will we go back to being our own best friend and stop being our

own worst enemy?

You would find it hard to believe what my ghetto eyes have seen,

Can't trust the man standing right next to you and it's hard to trust the

police.

I know they have a hard job and all of them are not bad,

When lives are lost through unnecessary force and aggression I think it's

sad.

Redrum is redrum,

We just celebrated MLKs anniversary and we are still waiting to

overcome,

Is the problem we don't matter to them or is it we don't matter to us?

The things I see going on with some people in this world will make a
preacher cuss,

You tell me to try to control my emotions and watch my language that's
not easy; when I look around and see my people dying, mothers crying
and the people who could make a difference constantly making up
excuses playing games, and lying.

Basically, it's the blind leading the blind,

Why don't we just face it, a lot of people have lost their minds?

Physical and mental health is wealth we teach young children reading

writing and arithmetic; we need to start teaching them to love

themselves.

We need to teach the people in our communities how to stand together

in solidarity, in unity at all times not just in times of war, in times of

peace too.

If we were on the same page and learned how to work together imagine

what we could do?

Instead, we get stuck on our differences why you don't like me and why I

don't like you then we wonder why we are not elevating and making

bigger moves?

As if the odds against us aren't already stacked; we are hell-bent on

completing the task of holding one another back.

How ass backwards is that?

Even trains know how to stay on the track.

I do believe we are kings and queens but the world is not going to take us

seriously if we behave like drama kings and queens.

When we show up our presence must illiterate greatness,

We must always project our voices and speak up clear,

Be brave at all times and never be a slave to fear,

Seize every moment and make the most of every opportunity to shine,

You are the keeper of your own castle of how your greatness is defined.

Only the strong survive in this hood, there are straws that can break a camel's back.

A lot of people lost their minds and never came back from crack..

Time is something you can never get back so spend it wisely.

You don't have to be a product of your environment,

You don't have to live up to their expectations,

You don't have to be another stereotype,

You can be the exception to the rule,

You can build a better mousetrap and let the world beat a path to your door.

Follow your dreams channel your inner greatness,

Don't just fly high like an eagle soar.

You'll Never Be Me

We are all stars, why can't all our lights shine?

You can't pay some people to support you,

But they sure will give you a hard time,

The audacity of some people,

That never think twice about crossing the line.

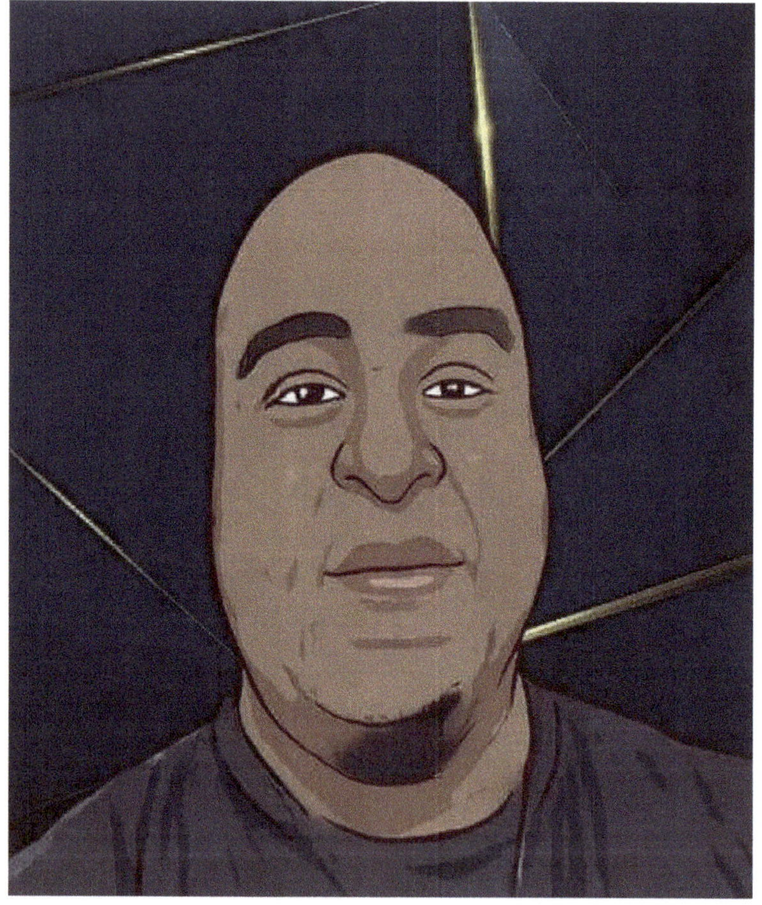

The main ones screaming loyalty,

Are the most disloyal over time.

Most people only stick around when it's most beneficial to them,

As soon as things appear to fall apart,

They get gone with the wind.

That's why I'm very careful who I let in,

My circle those who you let get the closest to you,

Be the main ones that hurt you.

I didn't get here riding coattails,

I got here paying my dues,

I bear my soul through my poetry.

Many times it's similar to singing the blues,

You can sample my lines but have you lived my life,

Have you ever walked a mile in my shoes?

I came out the wound kicking and screaming like a donkey,

You think you have had problems?

I strive to live my best life,

But sometimes situations get funky,

Trials and tribulations come fast,

Stopping you dead in your tracks like an 808,

And as if life isn't already hard enough,

You have to deal with unnecessary hate.

People find a reason not to like you for one reason or another,

We all supposed to be sisters and brothers,

Instead of working together we would rather undercut one another.

One minute we seemed cool,

I guess that was only your representative,

You was just playing a role.

Some of ya'll are so cold,

It's as if you have no soul,

The people who are meant to stay remain in your life,

The people who are not meant to stay in your life go.

You learn hard life lessons you move on and you grow,

You play the cards you are dealt and go with the flow,

Sometimes you think you know what people are capable of but you really

don't know.

I've been thrown out of better places and had much bigger fish than you

walk out in my time of need,

You just gave me another reason to write and make the ink bleed.

No more playing round,

Time to fix my crown,

You better ask somebody it's on and popping,

It's going down,

Better fasten your seat belt,

This mothership is about to take off.

I grab the mic and go off,

Why, because I'm a boss.

Like a groupie backstage, you get tossed,

You talk all that big talk,

But we see your yellow streak, man, you soft,

I bet you won't dare come outside and play after dark,

You better stay away from the open water go somewhere and build

castles in the sand,

If you don't want no smoke with the shark.

You can only fool some of the people some of the time,

Enough about this cat, pour me a glass of wine,

I got places to go and people to see.

Go find some more lines to bite, you still a sucker mc,

You are not the first and you won't be the last imitator to borrow from an

originator,

Imitation is the highest form of flattery,

You tried it but you'll never be me.

I Still Feel Your Frequency

A temporary disconnection still,

Cannot keep us from being connected.

You feel my strong energy,

The off and on button is not,

Functioning properly.

You try to write me off,

And turn a blind eye but you,

Are still locked into my frequency.

You feel the wave impulses,

Frequently,

You are miles away,

But our connection is so intense,

It's as if you are right beside me.

Can't run away from destiny,

Your mouth says your done with me,

I'm always on your mind constantly.

Here is where you really want to be,

I can read your mind,

I know the secret thoughts,

You don't want anyone to know,

You wanted me so bad it hurts,

You called yourself letting me go,

But deep down you never ever,

Let me go.

Although worlds apart our universes combined,

You may not talk about me,

But I'm always on your mind.

The type of connection we have,

Is so strong you ran away,

Because you were afraid,

Too bad we didn't get to lay,

Down in the cosmic bed that we made.

I could have spoken to your body,

I still speak to your soul.

Too bad you have been hurt so many times,

When a man seems too good to be true,

Your defense mechanisms kick in overdrive,

And you always let the best thing

That could have ever happened to you go.

I still see your face and hear your

Voice when I go to sleep,

This universal connection we have,

Like still waters run deep,

I bet you still dream about me,

I appear in your wildest fantasies.

Time passes on words go,

Unspoken,

All the remains are the memories,

Of what could have been,

An uncovered trench of emotions,

Left hanging wide open.

I still feel your frequency,

Your vibrations and wave impulses

Are strong, you feared Mr. Right

And chose Mr. Wrong.

Making love to him and,

Imagining it is me,

Ya'll have mixed signals.

And I'm locked into your frequency,

You are very convincing,

But I see through all the lies.

I know you still want me,

I can see it in your eyes,

When we engaged in deep

Conversations, verbal stimulation

A burst of energy ran through.

Your body and your soul,

Became energized,

Although we are miles apart.

I still feel your frequency,

I'm the one you let get away,

Forever being inside your wildest fantasies,

When we should have been reality.

He has your body,

But I still have the key.

Spring Time Has Arrived

The winter chill left,

Spring time is here,

The temperatures are warmer,

Flowers fragrances and pollen is in the air,

Insects are in a work,

Watch then swarm.

It's that time of the year when we get thunderstorms,

Grass is turning green, flowers are blooming,

Lightening is flashing, thunder is booming,

I love this season, mother nature is running high.

It's a clear blue sunny day,

There is not a cloud in the sky,

I'm loving the energy and I'm feeling the vibes.

Butterflies soaring such a beautiful sight,

A good time to take a vacation,

Go ahead and book your flight.

Stars and the moon shining bright at night,

Growing season is about to begin,

Make sure you tell a friend.

This is a wonderful time full of cheer,

Spring has sprung my favorite time of the year.

The Joking Elephant

The joking elephant loves playing tricks on everyone,

He's just getting started when you think he's done.

He's such a dirty little rascal,

He loves feeling in charge,

He's the king of his castle,

He thinks everything is funny he loves laughing.

You better have a good sense of humor,

Or your two personalities will be clashing.

You want him to chill out,

Keep on hoping,

He rocks in a chair until it's broken.

He plays so much, he leaves the door open,

This little silly elephant really needs to quit,

He turns everything into a skit.

He always acts like he is on a cloud,

He is so silly and he is proud.

If he was a child he would get plenty of spankings,

He's always getting into mischief and always pranking.

He should have been a hyena with all of that giggling,

He will find your tickle spot and never stop tickling.

The joking elephant will tell jokes until there are no jokes left,

He pushes the limits he will joke and laugh you to death.

I Look Nothing Like What I Been Through

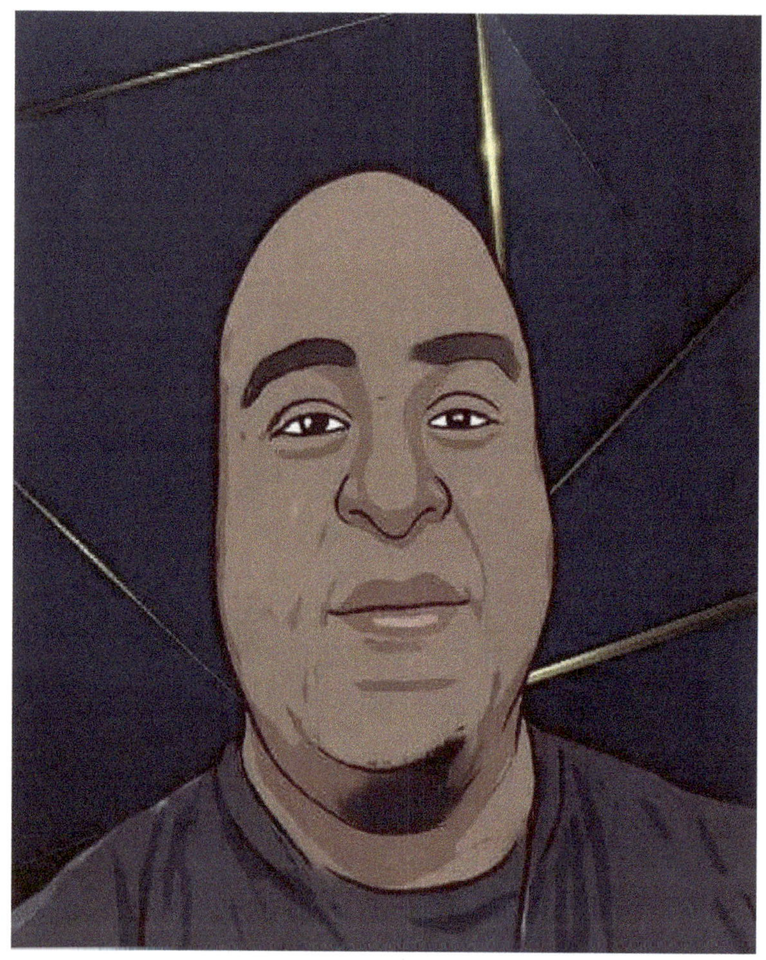

I've come so far from where I've been,

I count the hairs on my chin,

Those mistakes I will never make again.

I now have a clean slate,

Time to start my life over and begin again,

This time I want to get it right,

I made it through the long dark night.

I'm a man and I feel alright,

I've been through the bark and the bite,

Sometimes you have to fight,

It's all a part of life.

Through it all, I kept my head,

It's a miracle I'm alive I could have been dead.

I have so much to be thankful for,

I'm so glad God closed that chapter door,

Now I'm moving on full speed ahead.

Time to get this bread,

I'm on a mission, I don't have time to play,

This time, I'm going to do it my way.

I finally see the light,

Now, I get to rewrite a new chapter of my life,

I'm looking ahead not looking behind.

It's a brand-new day, it's my time to shine.

95

You're Are A Gift from God

I want you to remember each day you are special,

You are a gift from God,

 You are a blessing,

There is no one else like you.

You were created unique,

Wisdom pores out of you every time you speak,

Your words hit deep I see your face in my sleep,

You mean the world to me.

Such a ray of sunshine Such a source of motivation,

You are my hero and a source of inspiration,

I just want to give you your flowers before your expiration.

Each day I wish you safe travels to your destination,

May God guide you through your navigation,

I hope you make it through whatever unfolds,

Like the river my love for you still flows.

You are a very special person,

I just want you to know,

Keep this close to your heart.

When times get hard,

Never forget you are a blessing,

You are a gift from God.

BELIEVE IN YOURSELF

You have to believe in yourself,

Believe you can when others say you cannot,

Never give up.

Give every effort the best that you've got,

Don't let other people's words dictate your excellence.

Let your actions cancel their words,

You are more than enough.

If you keep working hard you will get everything you deserve,

I can a time when people told me I would never make it.

I took the advice of my uncle who said before I get there, fake it.

I played the role until my dreams became reality,

Your biggest determining factor is your mentality.

If you keep on pushing eventually something will move,

When others don't see the light,

You still have to keep believing in you.

If I had listened to the naysayers and nonbelievers,

Where would I be I'm glad I kept going.

I never stopped chasing after my dreams,

Keep paying your dues.

Doing what you have to do,

Sooner or later doors will open,

No will become yes,

Your gift will make a way for you,

The same ones who looked down on you,

Will have to look up at you.

A dream deferred will become a dream that has come true,

Don't listen to the negative voices,

Continue to believe in you.

I Wish You Well

Together, we stand divided we fall,

I wish success, liberty, justice, and good health for all.

I hope you find what you are looking for,

I hope you complete your journey and walk through that open door,

I hope it's everything that you are hoping for.

May you have happy birthdays and many more,

I hope you find happiness and unlimited joy,

I hope what you build no one will destroy,

I wish you well I wish you the best.

I hope you pass all of life's tests,

I hope every choice you make is in your best interest,

I hope you find peace and continue to be blessed,

I know you are capable of doing anything you set your mind to do,

I wish you well.

Don't get in the way of your dreams coming true,

You were created for a purpose,

You were made to be great.

Take a chance on yourself,

Step out on faith,

Find your calling,

Serve your purpose well,

We all have a story to tell,

I wish you well.

Wildflowers

Such a beautiful sight down here on the meadow,

The grass is green, it's late Spring.

Wildflowers are blooming in an array of different colors;

Insects and creatures are stirring,

The sun is shining it's a great day to relax and be lazy.

Clear blue skies not a cloud in site,

I'm enjoying a gentle breeze feeling all right.

The beauty of nature is refreshing,

Sweet smells fill the air,

It's a lovely day in the delta.

All is fair and I don't care,

Frogs are singing for rain,

Rabbits are hopping,

Positive vibes are popping,

Negative energy I'm stopping,

A beautiful day to enjoy the wild.

Today, I lived my best life in style,

While in the meadow I saw bumblebees hard at work,

Gathering nectar to make honey.

Hummingbirds flying it's a wonderful time to enjoy and cherish nature,

I'm lost in the moment free as a bird, this is a time I'll forever savor.

I Want to Be Innocent Like A Child

When we were children, we were innocent,

Little girls and boys,

All we wanted to do was play with our toys,

All we wanted was to be loved and we knew how to love,

Before we were pressured into being what society wanted us to be.

We were young, wild, and free,

I remember as a child I wanted to grow up and be an adult fast,

Now I find myself wanting to be a child again.

People don't want to get along,

I feel like I'm in the middle of a battle that I can't win,

Time is precious we should be cherishing our days,

Instead, it seems we are out here caught in the maze,

Caught up in the matrix how can this be.

We're not young anymore but we should still be wild and free,

It's way too many people out here starting problems,

We are adults we should be mature enough to move on and solve them.

Why we have to make life so hard?

Why we have to be another pain in the butt?

We should be encouraging one another so we all can elevate and come
up,

We say we don't want drama and that we want peace,

Yet we argue, fuss, fight, and hold on to grudges and beefs.

Where is the love, handshakes, and hugs?

If we are civilized adults, why do we behave like thugs?

Sometimes I just want to run away and disappear far away off of the

grid,

I want my innocence back that I once had as a kid,

The older I get, the more things go south.

If you don't have nothing good to say you should close your mouth,

Some people only open their mouth to say something bad,

All this wasted time and energy, the situation is really sad,

All of this tripping what's really going on?

We should be living life to the fullest doing it right,

Instead, it's too many people instigating and hating doing it wrong.

How can you say you want peace and not try to get along?

When you call me, I want to hang up in your face and unplug the phone,

If you are not talking common sense,

Leave me alone.

It seems like the days of people acting civilized are long gone,

These dogs just want to bring a bone and carry a bone,

Shame on these grown-ups keeping up all of this drama.

I know you was taught better than this from your momma,

You make things harder than they need to be,

If all you come to do is start confusion stay away from me,

If I can't have my innocence back, can I at least have my peace?

Down by The Creek

Down by the creek the water is flowing,

Stream is purifying and relaxing,

Frogs hopping by fish, swans, and snakes swimming,

Plants growing flowers blooming,

Everyone is winning.

It must have been like this in the very beginning,

When the world was first created in the age of the dinosaurs,

I can imagine how they would roar,

Then came the cave man living in the wild,

Living off the land cooking off wildfire,

Doing whatever it took to survive outdoors,

Must have been one big heck of a chore.

Seems like Deja Vu I've been here before,

The first humans lived without advanced technology,

We have today.

Imagine that and they were still ok,

They didn't have all of these illnesses and problems we face currently,

You had to know how to hunt in order to eat,

No one had to steal and rob,

Live off the land, protect and provide for your family that was your job,

Listening to the sounds of the creek,

Told me stories untold about an ancient land,

That has been stole, bought, and sold,

This land has seen many people come and go.

The trees still grow, and the water still flows,

So many things have went on,

Only God knows.

The spirits of our ancestors roam free,

Once upon a time when man and beast lived in simplicity,

Before automobiles and high fashion existed,

They did not have processed foods and biscuits,

They didn't have tubs they had to bath in creeks, rivers, and streams,

This place once existed that now only exists in our dreams,

We could learn a lot from this beautiful creek,

The answers we are looking for we will find if we seek.

I Am Edward

I am Edward a man, not a myth,

I write poetry it's my God-given gift,

I have a way with words,

My smooth voice can calm you down.

I was born and raised in the delta,

I'm from the Hell Town,

Where people will run you over like it isn't nothing,

If you are from where I'm from,

You would have a story to tell.

People would come on your porch and steal your mail,

My town was so small people would see you coming,

You had to come high or stay at home.

Poverty was widespread,

Bill collectors calling on the phone,

People trying to get theirs trying to take yours.

Summer heat so hot your sweat would pour,

You can take the man and woman out the ghetto,

Just remember the core is still the core.

Many days I was drinking that 40-ounce bottle,

I walked with a strut I would bobble and wobble ,

You couldn't tell me nothing when I was on that juice.

I was young, hardheaded, wild, and loose,

I had a tongue like a sword my words would cut,

Talk trash at your own risk,

I bet I would make you shut up.

We could get buck wild and fight I could give a damn,

If we tore the club up.

I got tired of people picking on me,

I became MC Lee he was a beast,

I didn't start nothing I wasn't prepared to finish,

I was a young bad ass like Dennis The Menace.

I was big like Brutus if you wanted it with me,

Popeye you better eat your spinach,

Anything you could do I could do better,

I was tough like leather and well put together.

People would try to roast me,

Make me the butt of their joke,

I made sure I gave them all of the smoke,

I would cuss them under the table,

I had no filter, I was cold.

You could get it regardless of if you were young or old,

I had my dark shades on people thought I was possessed by the devil,

I was on a whole other level,

I was ready for war,

Down for whatever,

These days I come in peace,

Don't get it twisted the core is still the core,

I'm still MC Lee,

I just go by Edward.

Big Mama

Things have not been the same since Big Mama has been gone,

I have been struggling to make ends meet so I can make this house a home.

Fish are not biting seems like my world has come to an end,

I can't find a job and I lost all of my friends,

Even stray dogs run away from me.

I can't even get the preacher to pray for me,

What is a brother to do whoa as me?

I miss her cooking and hospitality,

She always knew just what to say to me,

Everything turned when you went home to the Lord.

I feel like I'm about to lose my mind,

The people I thought I could depend on,

Showed their behinds,

How could I fall for the okey doke?

Everything I had went up in smoke,

Wondering have I been punked is this some sick joke.

I feel like I'm running around in a circle,

I'm going out looking worse than Steve Urkel,

This has to be karma or be a glitch.

What happened to my life, did I press up on a whammy?

I should have jumped in the ground too when they buried my granny.

The Cussing Grandma

Don't mess with grandma she doesn't take no mess,

She will not hesitate to put you in check,

You better let her be you don't want her to go that route.

If you make her upset, she will cuss you out,

She will call you everything but a child of God.

When grandma gets upset, she goes hard,

Let her cook her food and watch her cable,

If you disturb her groove, she will cuss you under the table.

Granny gets gangster get her upset she goes insane,

She will blow you away like a hurricane,

Better not get smart if what you are about to say is not good you better

hush.

She has the gift of gab that made Too Short, Ice Cube, and Ice T blush,

You'll feel like your head has been rammed into a wall,

Her explosive tongue impressed Dre. Dre, Eminem, and Snoop Dog.

She spits that fire that ignites controversy,

She made Marilyn Manson say Lord have mercy,.

One time she got so upset she threw a meat cleaver,

She made Ozzy Osbornc say Lord Jesus.

When grandma gets upset it will not go good,

The cussing grandma is from the hood,

She is smoking a blunt in the kitchen cooking beef stew.

She is as nasty as she wants to be like the 2 Live Crew,

She will blow your ship up out of the water,

You think your hard I bet she is harder,

She should be a rapper or a comedian with a mouth like that.

Her pants should be sagging, and she should be packing a gat,

I bet she plays bingo drinking a forty,

I bet she greets her homegirls with what's up shorty?

I imagine she was fast back in high school,

You don't want granny to act a fool,

She will embarrass you make you hide your head,

Chew you out so bad make you wish you was dead.

The cussing grandma is so doggone raw,

To have a mouth like that should be against the law.

It's A Lonely Road

It's a lonely road,

I'm on trying to find my way back home.

I looked around through the distance,

Many of my friends were gone,

One minute you hold others near and dear,

The next minute they leave.

I just need some time out,

I need room to breathe.

People say hurtful words behind my back,

At times I find hard to believe.

What tiny webs we weave,

I pinch myself to make sure it's not a dream.

Unaware of what the next moment will bring,

Hanging on by a thin string.

When heartaches and pain came on the scene,

Looking back at the crazy choices I made as a teen,

All water under the bridge a distant memory.

These days it's hard to tell your friends from your enemies,

People tell you anything to draw you in.

I've barely survived many storms by the hairs of my chin,

This game is not set up for me to win.

I try my best to avoid committing sin,

Then the devil and these people,

Pull me back in again.

The many ways they make you feel no good,

They only see what they want to see I'm misunderstood.

They hear the words coming out of my mouth,

But do they comprehend,

A war of words tensions building,

Here we go again.

If We Could All Live Happily Ever After

How did we become such a beautiful disaster?

If only we could all live happily ever after,

Another day another dreadful chapter.

Lately, everything has fallen into the crapper,

Society divided even family divided,

Nobody on the same page.

We hope for the best every single day,

For the worst we always brace,

I find myself asking when all of this madness will stop.

We are caught in the crosshairs waiting for the next shoe to drop,

We used to respect the next person,

Now we are at the next person's neck.

If we don't get our acts together and things don't get better martial law is

going to be put in effect,

When did it become ok to not behave properly?

When did it become ok to disrespect a person's husband wife and ok to

damage or steal someone's property?

We used to be such a beautiful society,

How did we become a society in ruins?

I know we were all taught right from wrong,

When did we stop caring about what we are doing?

There has to be a better way,

What happened to following the golden rule?

Treating others how you want to be treated,

Together we stand divided we fall.

If we are not going to follow the rules,

Law and order will not be needed,

The enemy will not have to come from the outside to attack us,

We will be our own enemy,

We will be destroyed by ourselves.

If we keep doing the devil's work,

We will be defeated,

We will destroy ourselves and everything else,

His assignment will be completed,

That will be the end of our chapter,

Then there will not be no happy ever after.

Some people throw the biggest bricks,

Yet are very sensitive to bricks being thrown back at them,

I declare people don't play fair,

See why I say this game is not set up for me to win,

When you do me wrong, I'm supposed to play nice,

Turning the other cheek,

Meanwhile you're supposed to have fair game.

Permission to make a mockery out of me,

I don't know what play book your reading from,

You must think I'm soft.

If you throw shots at me,

You can expect me to clap back,

I must go off.

I'm a very nice person,

I'm actually humble and meek,

Just because I'm a kind person,

Don't expect me to be weak.

I don't like going there but you took it there first,

So, I'm coming for your head,

I'm not going to hold it in because,

Pressure causes pipes to burst,

It's a lonely road,

When you are trying your best,

To make it up to the top.

If only everyday could be a good day,

If only finally all this foolishness and drama would stop.

Someone Give This Heart A Pen

I'm on this journey called life,

Still on a quest to get the love I once had back,

Someone please can you give this heart a pen,

I need to breathe and exhale again,

I need to get the magic back,

Relight my fire bring back the good times,

When the world was ours,

Can I get caught up in your rapture again?

Can we relive that special time?

When we were one and our souls glowed,

When we were like two peas in a pod,

Many tried to come between us,

Not one of them succeeded,

We stood together on the battlefield,

Our love was the protective shield.

We had the keys to each other's hearts,

No one else could ever make you feel,

The way you made me feel.

Someone can you give this heart a pen,

Can we fall back in love with one another again?

Please give me something real again,

It's too painful to pretend,

Give me back my sweet love and my best friend,

Please, God, no, don't let this be the end.

Cupid, please hit us again with your bow,

I'm willing to fight for our love,

I'm not ready to give up on us and let it go,

There has to still be something there,

I'll leave if you say it's over,

I'll stay if you tell me, you still care,

Someone, please, can you give this heart a pen?

Lord, only if it is in your will,

Make us fall back in love again.

Power in My Pen

My pen births revolutions,

I get clarity in a world full of confusion,

This is real not an illusion,

There is power in my pen.

I hold it like a sword,

I was given this gift from God.

If I manage to inspire one person,

I have done my job,

I put the pen to the pad,

This class is in session.

I write to enlighten myself and others,

Breaking the chains of oppression,

I feel like I'm a superhero,

As I write these bars,

Healing through poetry putting Band-Aids on scars.

Everyone has a past,

You would be shocked what goes on behind closed doors,

Left open wounds and sores.

I tear down walls I break through glass ceilings,

There are millions of others,

Who sympathize with my feelings?

Poetry is my healing,

Together we can open new dimensions if we are willing.

We came into this world innocent as children,

If we could learn to sit down at the table peacefully,

Imagine the masterpieces we could be building,

There is power in my pen.

A cup of tea for me to swallow,

My bridge over troubled waters,

Escaping tips that are hollow,

Living every day of my life,

Like there is no tomorrow,

Wherever the Most High instructs me to go I follow.

Feisty

She's an around the way girl,

She has a feisty attitude,

She has the lock and key to open the door to your deepest desires,

She has a mouth full of fire,

She will put you in check.

One thing she won't tolerate is disrespect,

Her disability does not define her,

Don't get it twisted,

She will not be intimidated,

You will not force her to kick it,

She will tell you about yourself,

Give you a verbal blistering,

Don't mess with her,

If you don't want to get your feelings hurt.

You will respect her,

She is a pit bull in a skirt,

She is really nice,

She is as sweet as a kitten,

She will be your best friend,

Just don't start tripping,

She will put you in your place.

You tick her off bad enough,

She will spit in your face,

You rub her the wrong way,

Her words cut deep.

You piss her off bad enough,

You better keep one eye open in your sleep,

She can be playful or serious as a heart attack.

If you get her upset, you better watch your back,

She is a wildcat that needs to be tamed,

She is full of fire,

You will remember her name,

She is feisty.

Strawberry Shortcake With A Cherry On Top

Come here strawberry shortcake with a cherry on top

You make my bells ring

I'm fully loaded and cocked

You're a sexy little mama

Do your thing don't stop

I'll put that thing in reverse

If I get my hands on you

I will put my love on top

I dig your style

You have a whole lot of flavors

You are my favorite dessert

Served with an appetizer and a chaser

You are one of the finer things in life

You excite and delight

You are sugar and spice

I want a serving of you on my plate

You are my wildest fantasy

I just can't wait

Why you have to play hard to get

We could take off like a jet

Have tons of fun guaranteed I bet

Strawberry Shortcake with A Cherry on Top

I'd like to make your shimmy, shimmy cocoa pop,

I'd put it on you hot, heavy, and risky,

Make you snap, crackle, and pop,

Just like rice crispies.

You send my rocket to the moon,

You have been a naughty girl,

Step in my room,

Let's walk on the wild side,

Let's have some fun.

Come on, sexy little mama,

Make my kingdom come,

Strawberry shortcake with a cherry on top.

Once I get my hands on you,

I'm not going to stop,

Until I make your shimmy do the cocoa pop.

If I Could Start Back Over

If I could start back over,

I would do it all over again.

I would change somethings,

Be more careful of the people,

I call my friends,

Can't trust everyone,

I see how bad somethings had to end,

Made me so mad the way it turned out,

Had my whole attitude on ten,

Had to fix my crown,

I came in this game to win.

Had to cut my ties with shady people,

They will screw you over again and again,

They will mess you up,

Treat, you like you are a fool,

Them are not your friends,

Doing stuff that is not cool.

Throw the whole friendship away,

Toss their tail in the pool,

They are with the same stuff,

That they were with up in school.

A snake is going to be a snake,

A leopard does not change its stripes,

How can you be my friend?

Doing stuff, I don't like.

If I could start back over, I would do somethings over again,

One thing I'd do different is choose much more careful of the people I

call my friends,

You know it is sad I had to lose before I'd win.

If I put myself in the same position,

They would do it all over again,

As you get older you get wiser you learn better,

When you know your worth,

You will refuse to settle.

How could you do me wrong?

Then laugh right in my face,

You didn't deserve to be in my life,

The best thing we did was when we went our separate ways.

In Memory of Peter Pan

I met this kind wonderful woman nicknamed Peter Pan,

She always made time to listen,

She would always be willing to give help and assistance,

She always would do the best that she can.

She had a heart of gold,

She loved the Lord,

She went all out for the ones she loved,

For her loved ones she went hard.

She was very sweet, but you had better not hurt the ones she loved or her

cubs.

If you crossed the line, her tongue was like a sword, and she would chew

you up,

She really could cook breakfast, lunch, snack, and dinner,

It sure did taste good her special recipes were a winner.

I really do miss her presence she knew what to say to calm you down.

Her heart was filled with love,

I'm sure right now she is with the angels and God up in heaven up

above.

Every time I see a red cardinal I think of you,

You changed me for the better now I'm careful of what I say and of what I

do.

May you rest in peace, Peter Pan,

This poem is in memory of you.

No more sickness, no more pain, no more suffering; well done your journey in life is through,

I could never thank you enough for everything you did for me,

You were a bridge over troubled waters.

Thank you so much for your Northern Hospitality,

Please watch over the family and me,

Say hello to my momma, daddy, and the rest of my ancestors for me.

As Long as I Have You

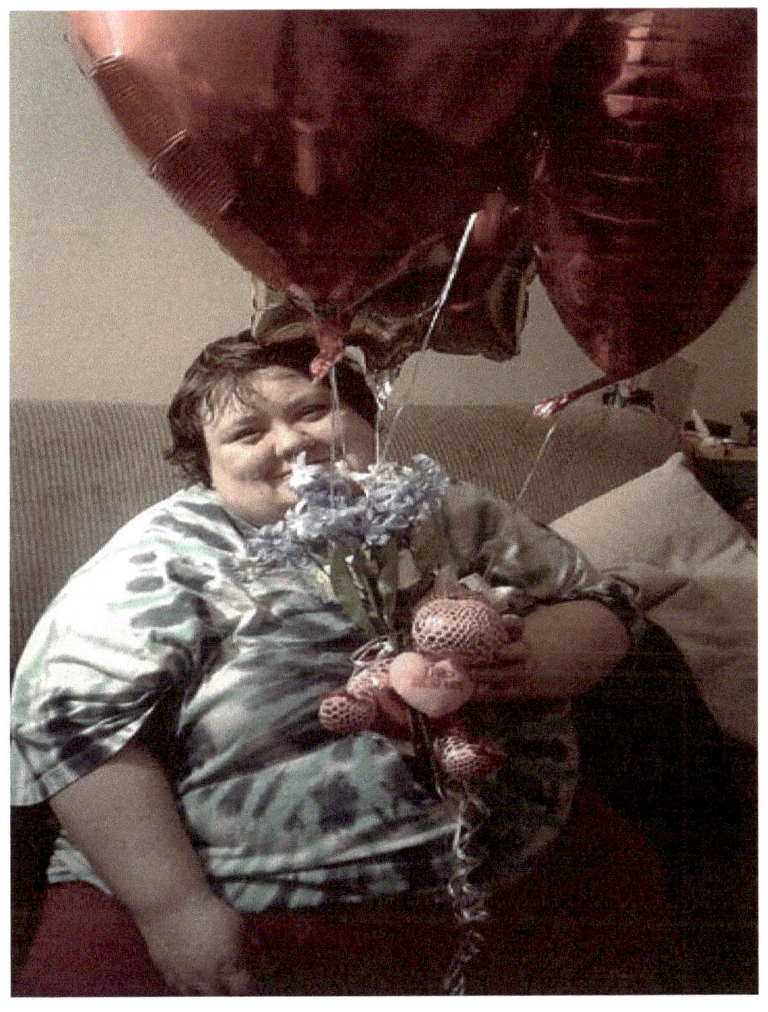

Roses are red,

Violets are blue,

Oh, my sweet boo,

How much I love you.

Such a breath of fresh air,

You make life worth living,

Every day you are by my side,

It feels like Thanksgiving.

You are my sweetheart, my lucky charm,

We are hand in hand and arm in arm.

My life would be incomplete,

If I didn't have you by my side,

You are my partner in crime,

Together we ride like Bonnie and Clyde.

If I was the student and you were the teacher,

I would be the teacher's pet.

Everyone did not want to see us together,

We had to fight for our love like Romeo and Juliet.

You are my full-course meal,

My apple pie.

Your love is the truth,

It's not a lie.

When I'm with you,

Through the clouds I fly,

Through the lows and highs,

One way or another,

 We get by.

It was destiny I met you and you met me,

Together we are a masterpiece,

In a world filled with mediocrity.

I was made for you and you were made for me,

You are my better half,

My missing link.

If you were to ever leave me,

My heart would sink.

We are love and devotion,

Poetry in motion,

I ride your high tides like a surfer in the ocean.

You make my life so much better,

When its rainy in climate weather,

You are my umbrella.

I'm so glad to have you boo,

A love that is true.

My roses are red,

My violets are blue,

I'm on top of the world,

As long as I have you.

When Life Gives Me Lemons, I Make

Lemonade

Look around you look at the mess that we made,

When life gives me lemons I make lemonade,

I can't let stress get the best of me.

The devil is a liar,

When my time is up,

I want to go to heaven,

I don't want my eternal soul to burn in a lake of fire.

Sometimes we all wake up on the wrong side of the bed,

Enemy of my soul you will not steal my joy,

I choose to smile instead.

There are gonna be storms,

I just remember storms eventually pass,

Troubles come I remember troubles don't last.

Everyone around me fussing, even the kids won't play in peace,

Devil you can take all of this confusion back to the pits of hell with you,

Positive vibes only please.

Everyone gathers around for drama like they smell something good

cooking,

I refuse to give up on my dreams,

I'm going to keep on pushing,

I'm going to be much stronger and wiser.

After this storm passes.

Isn't it amazing how life teaches us?

Lessons we were never taught in classes,

Sometimes you have to go for what you know,

Get out of your own way,

We are going to be just fine, trust God.

Stop worrying about what people say,

You can move mountains with a tiny mustard seed of faith,

Never forget you can do all things through Christ,

You will bend but you will not break.

Lilacs

Sweet smell of lilacs blowing in the summer breeze,

I reflect back on words of wisdom,

My ancestors said to me,

Giant sunflowers standing tall and proud in the sun with a smiley face.

The light wind blowing,

Natures gentle embrace,

The river is telling a story of coming of age,

It's another day in the country turn the page.

We are building our legacy,

Red tulips in bloom,

Yellow daffodils weeping willows singing,

Cows on the farms grazing,

Horses riding the circle of life is amazing,

Deer searching for water panting,

Life in the woods is enchanting.

I love spring and summer time in the country,

Watching the birds, bees, and trees,

I let my mind wander and get lost in the breeze,

Red roses, honeysuckle, raspberries in bloom,

Grapevines running wild,

Let's enjoy nature lets live life to the fullest right now.

My Black Labrador Retriever

I used to have fun with my Black Labrador Retriever,

His name was Mister Man,

We would go on adventures,

Walking all across the land.

He loved swimming in our drainage ditch,

He would jump in and go fetch the ball,

Every time I would pitch it,

We had so much fun roaming around in the cut.

If anyone messed with me,

He would bite them in the butt,

We stayed down with each other,

He was my very best friend.

I was sad the day he died,

The day his life came to an end,

I know he went to heaven.

I really hated to see him leave,

God had other plans,

This is in loving memory of my dog Mister Man,

 It was time for you to go,

Only God knows why,

May your soul rest in peace.

Mister Man continue to fly high,

Seems like yesterday I was a little boy having fun,

I was outside playing with my BB Gun,

I was riding on my bicycle,

Mom and dad were alive.

We were riding up and down the highway,

The speed limit was fifty-five,

We are not getting any younger,

We are actually getting older.

The rules keep changing,

Politicians have a chip on their shoulders,

It's like every single one of them,

Is trying to prove something,

They all promise change.

Take a look around do we ever get the change we anticipate coming?

Our expectations go down the drain,

We only get a little something,

They let us down we let each other down.

I guess that's karma what comes around goes around,

Lately, it has been a big chill on our world,

I have a sick to my stomach feeling,

I feel like I'm going to call earl.

Something is very wrong,

Something don't feel right,

I feel it in my conscious,

I have a hard time getting to sleep at night,

There is war and rumors of war,

All on the news.

If I could play the guitar,

I would sing the blues,

Where in the world are we going to?

Once we were highly intelligent individuals,

Now we look like a ship of fools,

It's like we are all being set up for the slaughter,

So, this is what they call the new world order?

Lately, things going downhill,

It just is not cool,

They should have never taken prayer out of the schools.

If you waste not, you will not want,

Maybe Donald Trump was right we need to drain the swamp,

Could the liberals be right and have a point, too?

Time sure is flying, what are the American people going to do?

I want to thank you all for your support.

Thank you all for sharing, buying, and reading my book.

I hope you are all blessed, inspired, and encouraged to press on through life's challenges.

Keep God first and continue to pursue your dreams.

Remember through Christ all things are possible!

www.ingramcontent.com/pod-product-compliance
Lightning Source LLC
LaVergne TN
LVHW052022210726

843527LV00010B/344